the
**EXTINCT
SPECIES**
collection

THE
QUAGGA

For a free color catalog describing Gareth Stevens Publishing's list of high-quality books and multimedia programs, call 1-800-542-2595 (USA) or 1-800-461-9120 (Canada). Gareth Stevens Publishing's Fax: (414) 225-0377. See our catalog, too, on the World Wide Web: http://gsinc.com

Library of Congress Cataloging-in-Publication Data

Green, Tamara, 1945-
    The quagga / by Tamara Green ; illustrated by Tony Gibbons.
        p. cm. — (The extinct species collection)
    Includes index.
    Summary: Describes the physical characteristics and habitat of the quagga, a zebra-like animal that lived in southern Africa and became extinct by the end of the nineteenth century.
    ISBN 0-8368-1595-5 (lib. bdg.)
    1. Quagga—Juvenile literature. 2. Extinct mammals—Africa, Southern—Juvenile literature. [1. Quagga. 2. Extinct animals.]
I. Gibbons, Tony, ill. II. Title. III. Series.
QL737.U62G75   1996
599.72'5—dc20   96-4997

First published in North America in 1996 by
Gareth Stevens Publishing
1555 North RiverCenter Drive, Suite 201
Milwaukee, Wisconsin 53212 USA

This U.S. edition © 1996 by Gareth Stevens, Inc. Created with original © 1995 by Quartz Editorial Services, 112 Station Road, Edgware HA8 7AQ U.K.

Additional artwork by Clare Heronneau

U.S. Editors: Barbara J. Behm, Mary Dykstra

Printed in Mexico

1 2 3 4 5 6 7 8 9 99 98 97 96

the
EXTINCT SPECIES

collection

THE
QUAGGA

Tamara Green
Illustrated by Tony Gibbons

Gareth Stevens Publishing
MILWAUKEE

Contents

Meet the
quagga

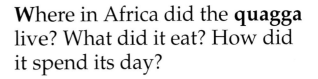

Where in Africa did the **quagga** live? What did it eat? How did it spend its day?

Was the **quagga** bold or timid? How large was it? Could it run fast? And why did it disappear from the planet? Read on to make many fascinating discoveries about the **quagga**.

The **quagga** had stripes on just half its body. It lived in Africa during the 1800s. Scientists called it *Equua burchelli quagga* (EK-WAH BER-CHELL-EE KWA-GAH). Sadly, the **quagga** became extinct toward the end of the 1800s.

You are about to go on an exciting time-safari, back to the age of the **quagga**.

The curious

If you had looked at the **quagga** from the front, you probably would have mistaken it for a zebra. It was the same shape as one and had stripes. But if you had looked at it from the back, it did not look like a zebra. A little way down the **quagga**'s back, the stripes began to fade. Farther down, the **quagga**'s coat became a solid brown color.

Settlers first came upon the **quagga** in southern Africa. They thought the partially striped creature was a female Burchell's zebra (now also extinct).

The **quagga**, as you can see from this illustration, was horselike in many ways. Its slim, hooved legs, for instance, allowed it to run energetically over the grasslands.

quagga

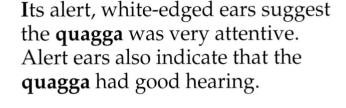

Its alert, white-edged ears suggest the **quagga** was very attentive. Alert ears also indicate that the **quagga** had good hearing.

The **quagga**'s tail was somewhat like a horse's, with long black hairs at the end. It must have been useful for shooing flies.

The **quagga**'s mane was striped and also fringed with black hairs. Its head resembled a horse's in shape, with dark coloration around the mouth.

Like the horse, the **quagga** was an herbivore, grazing mainly on grass. But even though it did not hunt other animals, the **quagga** would still fight back if another animal attacked it.

The African

The area of raised, open grasslands in which the **quagga** lived was known as the veld. It provided an ideal environment for the **quagga**. The climate was warm, and there was enough rainfall so that herbivores, like the **quagga**, did not have a problem finding places to graze on grass. They simply kept moving on to areas where grass was abundant.

The natural habitat for the **quagga** was mainly the area of southern Africa around the Cape of Good Hope. In 1806, the British captured the region from French, and then later Dutch, settlers. The area was ideal for farming. It was called Cape Colony. In 1910, it became a province of South Africa.

Life there was generally peaceful for the **quaggas**. Nevertheless, they could be threatened at any time by predators. As a result, **quaggas** would stay together in groups in order to protect the young.

A newborn **quagga** would not have been fast enough to escape the jaws of a lion or leopard.

veld

The sound of

It's sad that no one will ever again hear the sound a **quagga** makes. Unfortunately, the animal became extinct before humans had learned how to record sound. Only written descriptions of the **quagga**'s voice exist. The **quagga**'s name is known to be derived from its call.

Upon reaching the part of Africa where the **quagga** lived, early Dutch settlers first called this animal the *quahah* (KWAH-HAH). The name is an imitation of the noise the **quagga** made. Later on, the name was changed to *quagga*.

Most of the time, the **quagga** was silent. But, like many other animals, when it needed to warn other **quaggas** — and other creatures, too — about a predator, it would give its call.

Try saying *quahah* loudly. Repeat the word several times from your throat, and you probably will sound just like the **quagga** did!

the quagga

Facing danger

The wildebeest sniffed the air. It had picked up a scent and began to feel anxious. Could there be a predator on the prowl?

But now that it had picked up the scent of a predator, the wildebeest could not fall asleep in case danger approached. A couple of ostriches began looking around anxiously, stretching their long, S-shaped necks this way and that.

It swished its tail and shooed away flies that were buzzing around in the noonday sun. The wildebeest had been looking forward to a nap.

The ostriches were on the alert, in spite of the intense heat of a nineteenth-century African afternoon. They were always among the first to spot an enemy.

together

The ostriches knew instinctively that the wildebeest had picked up the scent of a predator. Grazing nearby, meanwhile, was an adult **quagga**. It seemed preoccupied with its meal, unaware of any danger.

For thousands of years, these three creatures — **quaggas**, ostriches, and wildebeests — lived in close proximity to one another.

Suddenly, the **quagga** lifted its head and leaned it to one side, listening intently. It had very good hearing and could be relied upon to pick up distant sounds that other animals could not hear.

The **quagga** now cried its unique warning call. *"Qua-haah! Qua-haah!"* it cried.

Their combined keen hearing, eyesight, and sense of smell provided a superb alarm system against predators.

In a flash, the animals were off. Others of their kind immediately followed. A large, hungry lion was indeed nearby, stalking through the African savanna. And the ferocious carnivore was after a large meal.

Training the

Early settlers in southern Africa needed to protect their livestock from nighttime predators. Jackals, for instance, were usually on the prowl for sheep, cows, and chickens.

Many farmers actually succeeded in training **quaggas** to act like guard "dogs." Not only would the **quaggas**, with their excellent hearing, call loudly at the approach of an animal predator or human poacher, they would also attack.

Quaggas could also be tamed. In the 1820s, **quaggas** were brought to England and harnessed like ponies to pull carriages. People must have stared at the strange sight of these partially striped creatures trotting around London's Hyde Park, their wealthy owner at the reins. And, unfortunately, humans had other uses for the **quagga**, as you will soon discover.

quagga

The quagga

behind bars

A number of officials at European zoos thought **quaggas** would make interesting exhibits for visitors. By 1858, however, the **quagga** was already quite rare in the wild. Despite this fact, the London Zoo received a gift of a **quagga** that year. The zoo awarded the donor the Zoological Society's Silver Medal in gratitude.

Zookeepers thought they would be able to breed **quaggas** in captivity. But these strong-willed creatures found life behind bars much too frustrating. After all, they had been used to running freely in the wild. Now, they could only pace around a small area. One **quagga** became so upset that it beat itself to death by banging its head against a wall.

Today, the only **quagga** to be seen in Europe is a stuffed specimen at a museum in the town of Tring in southern England.

How was the

At the beginning of the nineteenth century, huge herds of **quaggas** roamed the veld, or grasslands, of southern Africa. Settlers who colonized this area hunted the **quagga** mercilessly. After 1806, life for the **quagga** further worsened when the British relaxed the hunting laws. In addition, farmers wanted the **quagga** as a guard "dog." They also used its meat as food, not so much for themselves, but for their servants. Plus, they prized the **quagga**'s beautiful skin.

The **quagga**'s hide was not heavy, but it was tough. This made it very popular. It was used for bags and sacks because these needed to be as light in weight as possible.

quagga lost?

Soon, humans had killed off the **quagga** completely, mainly with guns. In 1878, the last **quagga** in the wild was killed.

Some scientists have a faint hope, however, that one day the **quagga** will return.

They think the **quagga** may not have been a separate species after all, but a subspecies of zebra. These scientists think that if zebras with poorly striped coats are bred with each other, this might result in the reappearance of the **quagga**.

Threatened

The **mountain zebra** of southern Africa, shown here, is also in danger of dying out. Unlike **quaggas**, which lived on the grassy plains, these animals live in mountainous areas. They have never been very numerous, but they were still killed by settlers for their meat and hide. By 1965, it was believed that only about seventy-five of these zebras were left.

The **quagga** is gone, but the **mountain zebra** has been a little more fortunate. It has become a protected species in the Mountain Zebra National Park in Cape Province, South Africa.

There is a larger type of mountain zebra, known as the **Hartmann's mountain zebra**. Scientists believe there are several thousand of them remaining. Since poachers kill them, it could also be in danger of extinction. The loss of a species happens rapidly, as it did with the **quagga**.

cousins

Quagga data

The **quagga** was a remarkable animal — no longer to be seen either in the wild or in any of the world's zoos or parks.

The **quagga**'s mane was beautifully striped and ran the length of its neck. The mane was tidy, short, and fringed with black hairs. At the top of the **quagga**'s head, there was also a short, tidy area of black hair.

It is, of course, the **quagga**'s markings — extending only half its length or less — that make this animal so unique. Slim stripes ran symmetrically down the front of the **quagga**'s face, and then out to the sides of the face. The nose and mouth areas had a darker color than the rest of the face.

Above the eyes, stripes formed an upside-down *V*-shape. Thicker stripes ran around the bottom jaw, neck, and upper body, before fading to brown along the back. The **quagga**'s underbelly was white.

At the end of its slim legs, the **quagga** had hooves like a horse. It was probably quite a good runner and may have used its legs to kick when defending itself or protecting its owner's property.

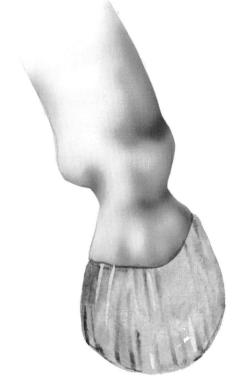

Toward the end of its thin tail, the **quagga** had a thick cluster of dark hairs that continued beyond the end of the tail. It is easy to imagine how useful this sort of tail must have been for shooing flies in the heat of southern Africa.

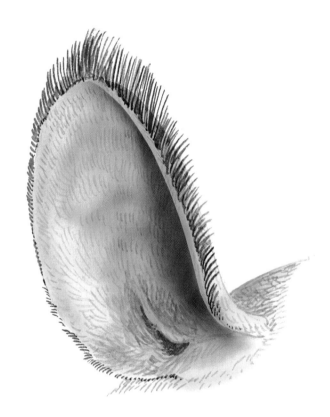

The ears were pointed and alert. The **quagga** had excellent hearing. If only humans had been alert to the need to protect the **quagga** before it became extinct!

23

Glossary

carnivore — a living being that eats meat in order to survive.

habitat — the area in which a plant or an animal lives and thrives.

Hartmann's mountain zebra — a large type of mountain zebra that is currently facing a threat from poachers. Only a few thousand survive in the wild.

herbivore — an animal that eats plants in order to survive.

mane — the long hair that grows from the neck and head of an animal, such as a male lion or a horse.

mountain zebra — an animal that lived in the wild in the mountainous regions of southern Africa. Because of its dwindling numbers, most have been taken to the Mountain Zebra National Park in Cape Province, South Africa.

poacher — anyone that hunts animals without permission.

predator — an animal that hunts other animals for food.

veld — raised, open grasslands with scattered shrubs and trees, especially in southern Africa.

Index